By John Ciardi

AN ALPHABESTIARY

DIALOGUE WITH AN AUDIENCE

AN
ALPHABESTIARY

AN
ALPHABESTIARY

JOHN CIARDI

Illustrations by

MILTON HEBALD

J. B. LIPPINCOTT COMPANY

Philadelphia and New York

For David and Jane Denker
And for Joel, Michael, Dana,
And (especially please) C. C.
From our house to their house
Ever fondly.

Author's Note

Fablers have always known that every animal is a moral waiting to be identified. Watch any animal: before long it will let you know something about mankind. It works the other way, too: watch any human being long enough and he will let you know something about which animal he might have been, given half a chance.

The other fact about fablers, of course, is the triumph of serendipity. They never really know which moral they are going to get to, but only that they will eventually get to one. Then, when it does come up, they think they knew it was there from the start.

AN
ALPHABESTIARY

A *is for ANT.*

*No one knows
how many Ants have stayed busy
how many years since the first
went into busyness, but any
estimate would produce a figure
something like a one followed
by pages and pages of
zeroes.*

*Whatever you do with
a figure like a one, it should
be clear, certainly, that zeroes
can go on accomplishing nothing
thereafter*

practically

forever.

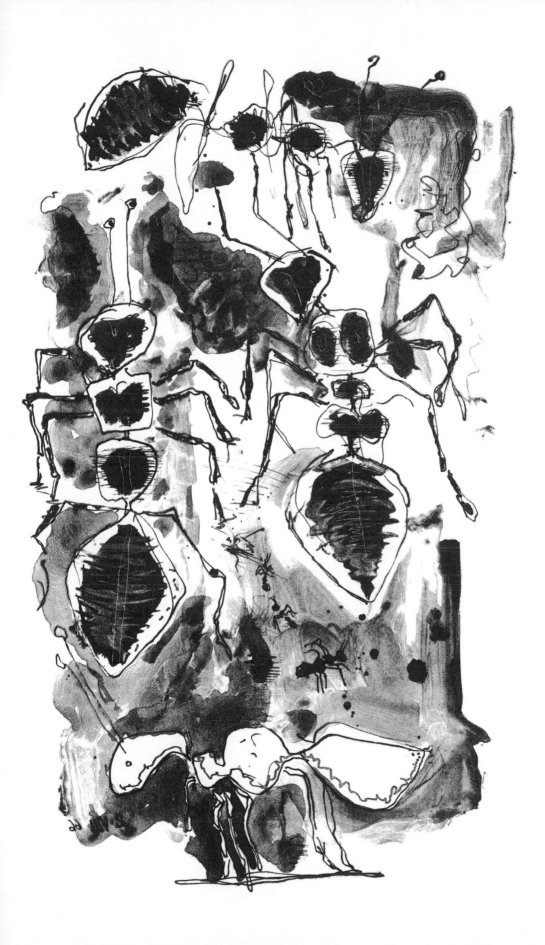

B *is for BOMBERS, our national pride.*
And also for BOYS who like Bombers to ride.
And also for BLESS in "God Bless Our Side."

B is for BAD (the Enemy) whom
we Bless our Boys' Bombers Bravely to Bomb.
And for BELLS we ring out when we welcome them home.

B is for BANNER, which proudly we hail.
For BLAST and for BRASS and for BURIAL-DETAIL.
And for BILLY and BUCK, who are studying BRAILLE.

C *is for CAMEL, a very right beast.*

So perfectly adapted is the Camel
that it endures with equal ease
the desert griddle and the mountain glacier.
Its dense lashes keep any speck
of sand or snow from its eyes.
It stores its own water. Its great
splay feet do not sink in sand,
and they grip securely on stone
and ice. The Camel can be ridden
or pack-trained. And it is practically
tireless.
            As a result of such
perfect adaptation, it provides man
with transport, water (in an emergency),
hair, milk, and (eventually) meat.

Now, children: what is a Camel right for?
and for whom?
                Once you have stated
your own thoughts, try to answer
from the Camel's point of view.

D is for DONKEY.
What the
Camel is to the Arab, the donkey
is to the Spaniard, though in less
detail. Sometimes
there is very little water
between one choice and another.
If you are given a choice
and must live with people,
try to be born a person.

E *is for EARWIG.*
Earwigs are not
imaginary in themselves but imagined
to be more than they are. There is
some such beastlet in every codification,
Law itself being made not of realities
but of secularized mythology.

Legally classified Forficulida *and distinguishable*
by its wing structure and its tail pincers,
the common European Earwig (F. auricularia)
was called by the Saxons earwicga,
which is to say "ear–beetle" or "ear worm,"
so named because it was believed
(erroneously, but when has that mattered?) to burrow
into the ears of men, producing afflictions
equal even to the effects of gossip.

It is as hard, without special instruction,
to distinguish the Earwig from related species
as it is to distinguish one defendant at law
from all others. Like most defendants, too,
the Earwig, once exonerated in legal Latin,
remains forever guilty in the mother tongue.

Be careful what names you allow to adhere to you.
Avoid going to Law. Or, when all else fails,
dig into your leaf-mold deeper than confusion.

F *is forever for FOX.*
                    No beast
falls so inevitably into the alphabets
of all tongues, though the letter for him
keeps changing. Fuchs, *he is in German (which is,*
of course, our own word for him before it became ours).
Volpe *in Italian.* Zorra *in Spanish.*
Renard *in French.* Puccha *in Sanskrit.*
And so on. Every time you see him
you look again and he is not there.
Or he has flicked his tail, as he does
through the alphabets, and become something else.
Every language claims his shifting name
as the word for one way of being wise.

If you covet such a reputation,
learn to create the illusion
of speaking his own language to every man
without leaving the same name on any two tongues.

G, also inevitably, is for the GNU,
or Wildebeest, technically an antelope,
but more like a horse in the rear end,
and more like an ox in the head and horns.

There is always some likelihood of confusion
in the animal kingdom, or in what we
expect of it. Considered either way,
you can always write to your Senator
for further information.

Who is more likely
to know how an ox-like mind may move
with the speed of an antelope leaving
to final view the rear end of a horse?

H is, reluctantly, for HUMAN, a word
derived from Latin homo, signifying "man,"
and, more aptly, from humus, signifying
"soil/earth," hence "of clay," but
more recently an adjective involving
a distinction that in turn involves
a slander of the higher apes, implying,
as it does, that Human primates
have evolved a more enviable position
than their cousins by shedding their tails
in order to be followed around
by a less visible conclusion.

I is, naturally enough, any author.

"I"

we say, employing the same character
for "Number One," and always capitalizing it
when we mean ourselves.

(The consequences
of which have been made clear.)

It might
have been well, perhaps, to let I stand for
Iguana, a creature of great antiquity, which,
having been spared the concept of I-ness,
has already been here some aeons before us,
and seems likely to be here at least as many
after.

(In whatever I-dea time is.)

J is, splendidly, for JOHN, my—
I repeat—my name.
                    Others, to be sure,
have attached themselves to the same
sound and have insisted on being
identified by it. None, however,
has plumbed the infinite–true–secret
identity of John-ness in quite
the way I know all about.
                    John
(can you fail to see?) is I. Begins
with, is the name of essential I-ness.

In Italian, in fact, J is I-lungo,
as Y is I-greco.
                    It is exactly
that long I my name is, as you must
finally be made to understand
if you mean ever to have your own
name. I mean truly have it.

K is for KANGAROO, of which there must be
at least one pair in every zoo, whereafter
there will be several, and then several more,
and then again several more, until the surplus
must either be sold or shot.
                              Do not
take the Kangaroo lightly. He may appear
generally ridiculous when trained as a boxer
for side-shows, but how would you look
that far out of your habitat and jabbing
at local boobs for a living? And even so
expatriated, when was it ever the Kangaroo
that was carried out at the end?
                              Ungainly as
it may seem, it can move with astonishing speed
in a series of racing-dives from the spring-board
of its own hind legs. Gentle as it generally is,
it can turn, seize a dog in its forearms and
claw it precisely to dogburgers with the nails
of its rear-thumpers, supporting itself on that
impossible tail as it does so. Improvident as
you may take it to be, no other beast puts quite
so much in its pocket quite so inoffensively.

Kangaroos seem to have originated in Australia where they were generally successful for some aeons before it turned out that the grass on which they had been feeding was legally claimed by sheep and cattle. They are now, therefore, hunted both for sport and for these more recent views on legal distribution. Fortunately for the hunters, the flesh of the Kangaroo is a desirable venison. Under the right circumstances, therefore, you may chew on a satisfactory Kangaroo steak as you reflect by the campfire on the problems of population control, on the unreliability of outward appearances, and on the nature and consequences of redistribution since whoever was supposed to inherit what earth.

L is for LOVE, toward which all beasts
move in their season. Tooth and claw,
beak, hoof, and horn, come to Love's feasts,
stand guard upon it, stand in awe
of Love's wet fruit. On peaks and shores,
in nest, bole, warren, fold, or den,
and whether in or out of doors,
Love moves to Love. True, now and then,
some beast of its all-scalding blood
maims what it mates. Panthers are one,
and ferrets one, and man another. Still the good
of Love is seen—is seen and known—
in some part by all natures. So
the she-herd licks by the lone bull
its spindly young who, thus loved, grow
their sacs of flaps, their coats of wool,
tended by love, guarded by hate.
So in the wolf-den two or three
sharp puppies play till it grows late
and then run, ravening, to be.
So hawks and doves sleep in one tree
whose trunk, taken symbolically,
is Love. Whose roots, as we may see,
are hate. And so for you. And so for me.

M is for MOTHERS, who are, above all,
useful. Preferably, to be sure, married,
but in any case indispensable.
Motherhood can, we understand, be carried
too far. As can the attitudes
toward it. Some Mothers are harried.
Some are placid. Some beget feuds.
Some, harmonies. Some could
be called loose. Some are prudes.
Mothers, that is, are various. It is good
to have a Mother; to have had one,
inescapable. Motherhood would,
I daresay, command the respect of many
more clinicians were the prerequisites higher.
(It can, after all, happen to almost any
girl.) It is reasonable, I suggest, to admire
individual merit as it occurs
rather than the category. Inquire
of Eve, in reason, what is truly hers,
and of Lilith, hers. And so on.
Then, in proportion, as love measures,
love a bit more, and gladly.
Mothers are good to have, but if everyone
kept his, things would go badly.

N *is for NANNYGOAT—the silly*
who finds her loved one in a Billy;
while he, poor fool, without demur
finds all his dream of love in her.

With this much said, my fable ends.
Go look at your own married friends,
or look at your own wife at home,
and write your own end to my poem.

O is for OX, by which word we
signify what was meant to be
a bull, but suffered alteration.
Husbands, in late meditation,
may find some parable in this
all-hauling beast that does not miss
what it is missing.
                    The real joke
played on the Ox is not its yoke,
nor yet the spiking of its spoke,
but its name, which comes, we learn,
from German ochse, drawn in turn
from root words meaning "to make wet
[the female]"—that is—"to beget."
—What? Humor in the alphabet?

Words betray us. But the ox
is safe in this: it seldom talks.
A mercy—should it learn its name,
even it would blush for shame.

P is for PORCUPINE, a creature
subject to some debate, but though
sharp in rebuttal, never the first
to argue. He does not, as some say,
sling his quills. A placid logician,
he yields his points only when pressed.

Although he is a rodent, his name
signifies "spiny pig." Men, clearly,
have divided in their chosen views
of him. Witness, as one of many
divergent opinions he has engendered,
his various standing in Upper New England:
Vermont pays a bounty on his nose;
New Hampshire, on his ears (it may be
the other way round, but in any case,
how many of us are redeemable at death
in two jurisdictions?); and Maine
has seen fit to protect him as the one
edible, substantial, and common meat
a man lost in the woods can kill readily
with nothing but rocks, or a club.

Ah, what it is to be misunderstood!
But we all have our problems. If yours
is a tendency to get lost in the woods,
move to Maine and live on porcupine,
but save the noses for Vermont
and the ears for New Hampshire.
                                        Or is

it the other way round?

—No matter:
the thing about beasts (when we are not
hungry) is that they suggest possible
metaphors to us, and (when we are)
that they are good to eat in exact
proportion to how hungry we are. And
especially so if we can avoid
certain, likely, sharp consequences
in persuading them to our chosen view.

Q may as well be for QUEEN,
        the feminine of King, and sometimes
of Prince.
            There have been many Queens
in history, and some of them
have been anything you care to
imagine.
            There are fewer now,
and they require much less imagination.

Some are still profiled on money
but all have suffered some devaluation.

Time is inflationary.
                    It is easier
to put one's face on money
than to keep money up to face value.

R is for RAT, the noise in man's wall.
Wherever man goes, in no time at all
his Rat will be heard at work in the dark.
It is written that Noah took on his ark
two beasts of each kind to Mount Ararat.
But surely genetics knows better than that:
though Noah took no more than two Rats aboard,
it's certain that what came ashore was a horde.

The moral of which is—with all due respect—
don't start saving worlds till you learn to select.

S is three gray SQUIRRELS at a Mayday
in themselves (though it's November now)
pinwheeling in that beech.
                                    I may
never again see this world played so fast so
glad. Dante's angels at God-spree
round themselves round whatever tree
grows that high, could not be
sooner.
              Bliss, I think, is just this
squandering of energy that forever replaces
itself.
              Here, or There, it is
being able that blesses.
                                    Thoughts are carcasses
that can still see: as I sit here (slow,
fat, in the cadaver I shall go
nowhere in, as far as I know,
at no pace to nothing) and reach
for angels because three Sun-wound
gray Squirrels in that beech
chase one another's tail around
their perfect lack of idea—so caught
in themselves, so flung, so slackly taut
with everything they are that I am not.

T, the TURTLE, has been a long time coming
through everything, including fablers and
logicians. Aesop had him outrunning rabbits
(a likely story,) and Zeno proved that Hercules
could not overtake him because however fast
the hero ran, by the time he came to where
the turtle had been, it would have moved on.

What is this professional passion to speed him up?
Do we resent what sets its own pace? Wise Hercules,
unable to catch him by logic, simply overtook
him, and class was dismissed.
                                    The fact is
that even with logic on his side, he is
slow. He means to be overtaken.
Then he stops being and becomes a box.
It's a trick he learned from the egg:
hatched from a shell, he returns to it.
There is less to fear in not being born.

Nevertheless there is no reason
for taking him too lightly.
What if he does go nowhere?—he travels
without leaving home. He is ugly,
certainly—but how long has it been
since your last beauty prize? Remember, too,
the turtle takes revenge: when savage boys
carve their initials on his back, he waits,
goes off, then waddles in fifty years later.
"Look at you now," he says. And there you are.

Mock the turtle if you will:
armor is its own species and survives.

U is for UNCLE, a parent's brother
or aunt's husband, as the case may be.
Uncles are much like one another,
and often boozy. What children see
of Uncles is huge and full of jokes
and sometimes good for half a dollar.
Though twenty years later the old soaks
are not at all funny and seem much smaller.
Uncles are extra and fun to begin,
but when you grow up, they're not quite kin.

V *is for VICTOR, the beast that includes*
most of the rest when their meeting concludes.

If you are a natural loser, shun
surprising encounters, or learn to run.

W, the WEREWOLF, like many another
fragment of mythology, is no lie
but a transposition of impulse to
legend. "Manwolf" the name signifies.
And if there is no such wolf, there are,
certainly, such men under every moon
we entirely waken to.
                        Who does not
remember lying lit by his change
to first dark, his mind already loping
through a forest like home, while the scruff
thickened, and low in the throat
his name began to form?
                        We do
change back with a shrug at last,
but it is not for nothing we left
in the first place, knowing our way
wherever we went to dark tangles,
feeling the scent and our pace quicken
as we closed on that certainty
one shadow beyond us forever.

X is for interseXion,
the point at which any two
trails meet. If, for example,
a skunk leaves a strong trail
running roughly northwest,
and a bobcat crosses it
from, roughly, southwest, X
marks the spot at which
the bobcat in all probability
continues on its own course.

If, on the other hand, the trail,
even though it be somewhat
weaker, is left by a lamb, X
will almost certainly mark a
change of course for the bobcat.

It is not so much the emphasis
you place on your passing
as the invitations you suggest by it
that may create a following.

Y *must, of course, be YOU. Thank you
for having stayed through the assertions
of my I-ness. How could I have justified it
except in open exchange for your
You-ness?*
*You and I are in this
together, whether we say it or not.*

*In possibly spurious language
I might say, "The function of I is You."
—Meaning, in a possibly genuine sense,
that unless you have the function of your
You-ness, I have nothing to witness
to you, and have (though happily enough)
been passing my time whittling
no more than shavings.*
*So be it—
as some men play golf, I shall call this
my exercise. As with golf, to take it
seriously would be absurd, and not to take it in
some way would be to forego too many a good
walk nowhere.*
*In this sense, you are
an aspect with which I play, caring nothing
for the score, and gladly begging to be
conceded all putts, as I concede yours—
which is to say, in self-seeking generosity.*

Z *is not for zebra, but for Zoology.*

Since the present effort has been to achieve
the inclusive view rather than any
particular stripe, I must be firm on this point.

Habit, of course, has its own beasts and will cling
to them, but perception concerns all zoa.

Therefore, Zoology, it being the science
most like a looking glass, to teach us
resemblances, when we learn to face them.